WOODSMOKE

Books by Mary Summer Rain

Nonfiction
Spirit Song
Phoenix Rising
Dreamwalker
Phantoms Afoot
Earthway
Daybreak
Soul Sounds
Whispered Wisdom
Ancient Echoes
Bittersweet
Mary Summer Rain's Guide to Dream Symbols
The Visitation
Millennium Memories
Fireside
Eclipse
The Singing Web
Beyond Earthway
Trined In Twilight
Pinecones
Love Never Sleeps
Tao of Nature
Woodsmoke

Children's
Mountains, Meadows and Moonbeams
Star Babies

Fiction
The Seventh Mesa

Audio Books
Spirit Song
Phoenix Rising
Dreamwalker
Phantoms Afoot
The Visitation

WOODSMOKE

Autumn Reflections

Mary Summer Rain

HAMPTON ROADS
PUBLISHING COMPANY, INC.

Cover concept by Mary Summer Rain
Cover design by Marjoram Productions
Cover photograph by Digital Vision

Hampton Roads Publishing Company, Inc.
1125 Stoney Ridge Road
Charlottesville, VA 22902

434-296-2772
fax: 434-296-5096
e-mail: hrpc@hrpub.com
www.hrpub.com

If you are unable to order this book from your local
bookseller, you may order directly from the publisher.
Call 1-800-766-8009, toll-free.

Library of Congress Cataloging-in-Publication Data

Summer Rain, Mary, 1945-
   Woodsmoke : autumn reflections / by Mary Summer Rain.
       p. cm.
   ISBN 1-57174-373-1 (alk. paper)
   1. Meditations. 2. New Age movement. 3. Spiritual life--New Age
movement. I. Title.
   BP605.N48S865 2003
   299'.93--dc21
                                        2003012483

10 9 8 7 6 5 4 3 2 1

Printed on acid-free paper in the United States

To Love

WOODSMOKE

Betrayal can only come from those
you've loved or trusted.

We are one with all Living Energies.

Religious dogma can be an oppression
that begets fear.

Life Sorrows can be as a gentle death
that resurrects one to Life anew.

Living cells of every kind
have a consciousness
of living cells of every kind.

Following your own unique path by way of Unconditional Goodness and Love places the Golden Grail within one's hands.

To gossip is to voluntarily expose one's lack of wisdom and integrity.

A blessing a day, given away, brings joy
to the heart in a glorious way.

Until Destiny's appointed time—two measures beyond the outstretched Wingspan of the Risen Phoenix—the silent, sacred place below will remain as a gentle Heartbeat of Life Eternal beneath the funeral shroud of the screaming, burning place above.

Greatness is achieved
through the integrity
of spiritual simplicity—the *living* of It.

When the qualities of Wisdom profusely grow
within one's heart as a mountain meadow full
of wildflowers, each day rises as a fragrant
prayer to the Divine.

Your cleverness and great skill
is an amazement to me.
How is it that you can so easily
stand before a mirror and,
without guilt, look into the
reflection of your own eyes
after spending a day casting stones?

New Age is a term that many fear because they don't understand that it equates to the beautiful blend of physics and spiritual consciousness. Many characteristics of New Age elements dissolve the seeming paradoxical dilemmas of quantum physics.

All of Life courses along interconnecting
threads of the web of consciousness.
    Consciousness is intangible—of Spirit.
The Consciousness of the Creatrix touches
everything and is the breath of all Life.

The Causal Forces for one's ultimate Pathway through Life are not directly contingent upon the Impetus of the individual's personal desires or decisions, but rather upon the beautiful and nebulous Promptings of the wise Spirit Within, Which is ever acutely aware of Its Purpose.

Consciousness is the binding Tao
of all matter and non-matter alike.

Only the Fool says that Nature does not, cannot, weep.

Just because Nature does not speak the human tongue—does not form verbal words—does not mean it lacks a communicable language of its own.

Mortals are merely ignorant—deaf to Nature's exquisite language, her ancient Wisdom of the Ages.

Be not insensitive or numb to Nature's many facets for I say truly that the tree, the stream, the stone are *alive* with power!

Fear represses potential.

In order for Life to have shadows
it has to have light.
Which one you're drawn to is up to you.
You have a choice.

Why do you seek after *new* unknowns
when the knowns you currently believe in
are fragmented and not yet whole knowns?

Question not the motives of others
before those of self have been examined
and thoroughly understood.

He did not *die* for our sins.

He *suffered* for the Truth and lived on.

Wrapped in his shroud did he live on

    As blood still flowed forth upon its fine

        fabric

    Whilst his heart beat strong within the

    Healing linen of aloe and myrrh.

This the cloth does prove along

    With the deception and great fear of

    Discovery by current religious leaders.

Let your faith be not blind lest you

    Be led as lambs from the reality of it.

See you not a heretic in me but

    Rather cast your eyes upon those

    Others who were and are your deceivers.

For it is here you've heard the speaking

        That cannot be restrained.

I see your beaming pride when displaying your great quantity of collected shards of knowledge. Yet among your prized piles of pieces I observe not a single vessel . . . whole and unflawed.

Be not opinionated in your
definition of greatness.
Greatness wears not a sign
announcing its existence.
Greatness is a Silent Indwelling.

Twisting Paths
Unexpected Byways
Beckoning Waysides

We take subliminal notice of the whispered urgings and we are restless beings until we act on the compelling directives within. We then move to the sweet sound of our own metered chanting. We drift along the warm current of our flowing Spirits and, in gentle Acceptance, do we set foot upon the twisting paths, the unexpected byways, and the beckoning waysides.

Lock not your beliefs
in a box forged by others.

For those who walk in false wakefulness, the timbre of Truth's voice is heard as a distant and indistinct echo and, the meaning of Truth's words are remembered as a dream . . . fragmented and foggy.

In reality there is no emptiness, for all the
spaces are full and pulse with Life.
Spaces are merely the magic of an illusion—a
delusionary hallucination.
Reality's spaces are a Nothingness to those who
cannot see.

The Mind is bruised by rigid thought as it continually bumps into self-defined barriers. Rather, perceive with the fluidness of water that freely flows through crevices and around obstacles to explore and experience that which is beyond the obvious and is known as Potentiality.

In the beginning was the Word.
Alive
Immortal
Immutable is the Word still.
What makes you think
it ever departed from that?

Rudeness is self-gratification for those who lack Acceptance and Tolerance.

The Knowing and rigid thought
cannot simultaneously dwell
within the house of one's consciousness.

Consciousness is not dependent on the intake of breath nor the beat of a heart.

Consciousness is the mutable Life Force of every one aspect of the All That Is.

I hear the terms "sacred place" and "sacred object" and I am bewildered.

What means these?

Why is your sight so selective?

See you not the Sacredness within all things?

Thirst not for fine wine when
water is thy sustenance.

Oftentimes the greatest gift comes as a
word of encouragement, a helping hand,
or a warm and sincere smile.

Predictions are predictable
when following the
natural course of
the Domino Effect.

In slow motion,
Time slithers about me.
   Around and around,
   In an ever-widening circle,
   Forever seeking its tail
   In a futile search for self.
      Linear movement.
      Chronological thought.
While I,
   Beingness centered in
   the Eternal Moment,
   Wonder why?

Gentle Wisdom made her descent and,
finding no Companionship save her Angelic
Consort, dwelt unrecognized among the
throng of searching Souls.

The Earth's populace is as an innocent lamb playfully romping among the meadow flowers . . . completely unaware of the hidden wolves controlling what the innocents are told.

There are Realities existing outside thought—yet human thought has yet to envision them.

Philosophers say that jealousy is instinctive.
They are mistaken.

Many Paths appear to be correctly marked. They are cleverly disguised with all the seemingly appropriate signs, yet a nebulous, silent beckoning leads you in the opposite direction and you follow your inner promptings.

Many Roads are smoothly paved.
They are bordered with the fresh scent of vibrant dew-flecked flowers. They literally reek with the delusion of sun-drenched valleys and are filled with the hypnotically compelling essence of Love that attempts to draw you forward. They are but masterful Illusions. They are a contrived device to mislead and tempt those Souls lacking perseverance and clear vision.

Life is a cyclical journey of becoming.

Knowing what you don't know is Intelligence. Acknowledging what you don't know is Wisdom.

The Spirit's Consciousness is as a pearly Nautilus—a many-chambered Entity floating effortlessly through the Etheric Sea, propelled solely by Will.

Unconditional Love is the breadth
and depth of pure Spirituality.

Beware of those who claim the pursuit of expanded knowledge and intellectual inquiry to be a dangerous or heretical quest.

There is no question that is forbidden to ask.
No concept banned from exploration.

Interconnectedness is the Web of Life
is the Universal Consciousness
is the Divine Prime Intelligence.
All—One and the same.

The Knowing,
incorruptible and immutable
in It's purity of existence,
is . . . What Is.

Consciousness is not confined to the
persona of the Human Self but is expansive
in its
reach to be felt within the wayside weed, the
dolphin, the distant star.

I am never alone.

Within the woodland depths where lances of shimmering sunrays spear down through the jade and emerald greenery, my hearing perceives the hushed brush of air from its brilliant, miniature wings as they silently rise and fall.

I turn not to the delicate entity that softly alights upon my receiving shoulder, for the gentle Breath that whispers its ageless wisdom does breathe exquisite visions behind my eyes. The Butterfly Being is always and ever a truly welcomed and frequent companion along the woodland wayside.

I am never alone.

Within the ebony forest shadows of the deep alpine Night, there is never darkness surrounding me, for existing within the velvety blackness, like dancing fireflies, the living lights come to flicker about and encircle me.

Always there are companions.
Never am I alone.

Truth is That Which Is—the Unnamed—
the Gnosis, The Knowing that flows
through the living consciousness
of every cell of All That Is
issuing forth from
the Source of the Divine Intelligence.

The Apocalypse is an individualized
personal event that is unaffected
by linear time and is not chained to
any specific date or historical era.
It is not of a material world.

Solitude within Nature
has a subtle nuance of rarified air
that I cannot precisely define other
than calling it dignity—a divine dignity.

I pray that I have tread
gently through this Life.
I pray that my worn and tattered
moccasins have left subtle
footprints across the paths
of many. And
I pray that other travelers do not
strive to follow my trailing
imprints, but rather
they glance down now and then
along the way and simply
take note of my passing.

May your moccasins cross
the threshold of Truth,
And may your trail lead
into the Beauty Beyond.

Left speechless by the enchanting serenity
that emanates from the profound
Divine Presence found within all of Life,
I'm oft overwhelmed and engulfed
by the tranquil Garden of Sacred Silence
where the only words heard
are heartsounds.

Truly profound experiences
fill one with enduring humility.

To revere the created and not the Creatrix
is to live a contradiction.

Rather than striving for
the attainment of perfection
or its pursuit in all things,
strive to fulfill your individual potential
contained within the bounds
of circumstantial limitations.

Perfection is an attribute
belonging solely to the Divine,
and doing our best
is perfection in Her eyes.

Within me You've instilled Acceptance
and given me Patience.
You've mellowed me
and gifted me with solace.
In solitude, You are my companion.
In darkness, my eyes.
Never failing.
Always caring.
Sophia.

The spark of Intuition
is extinguished by thought.
Intuition is a call to Act, not analyze.

Reality is like a beach that alters
after the ebb and flow
of each wave passing over it.
Each wave, a new probability
that enters to alter the composition
and design arrangement.
The pattern, constantly changing.

Like a thief in the night,
fear of tomorrow steals away
the gift of today.

Those closest see me not, while those seeing from afar have seen.

This, the difference between seeing with one's eyes and seeing through The Knowing.

There's a reason why Love is blind and that reason is to keep it unbound . . . free. Its expression is, therefore, unhampered by an attendance to social status or mores. It hears not the ramblings and rantings of the self-righteous religious taboos and it sees not a confining distinction of race or gender. Love is free to be; it just *is*.

Love . . . just . . . is.

With only a slight shift in perception,
perspective transforms the ordinary
into the sublime.

I wonder why society has the idea that an individual perceived as a "saint" is a rarity when our whole world should've evolved into an entire civilization of saintly people by now?

Saintly behavior is none other than the daily practice of Unconditional Love and Goodness and, therefore, should be the norm rather than a rarity.

This old body is but a vessel for my
Spirit's Light—a lantern encasing It.
Upon my death the Light will be set free
to shine forth . . . without obstruction.

Sitting in the quietude of the fragrant piney forest, All That Is swirls within me. From behind closed lids I watch Life dance with wild and innocent abandonment and feel its sweet breath whisper upon the surface of my soul, "You are the universe." And after losing all sense of self, what is seen from an altered, new viewpoint is a pulsating Universe hovering ever so gently above the forest floor. Every living cell is a shimmering Cosmos unto Itself.

Along the path to The Knowing,
all paradoxes cease to exist.

All of Nature
is an expression of Divine Consciousness.

Intelligence is not the same as common sense.

The skeptic, so full of smart reasoning,
unkowingly displays ignorance
with smug aplomb.

Making fun of others shows people that you have a need to stroke your own ego, not to mention the blatant Rudeness it exposes. In other words, when people make others the butt of their jokes, their own Ignorance is hanging out for all to see.

The great, living Web of Life pulses with the influencing energies of every Life Cell of each living Species. Our energies affect the Nature surrounding us just as the emanating essences of Nature affect us. We are all cells of the living, Divine Consciousness. We are . . . each other.

The great, vibrational hum of Life—
the music of the spheres—
creates a pattern of eights
upon eights . . . the Double Helix.

The deepest serenity comes from
spiritual maturity and wisdom.

With Wisdom should one pause along the wayside to contemplate upon that which you wish to attain, for not all byways are hospitable inroads.

With Prudence should one pause upon the threshold of a new path to contemplate upon that which you wish to accomplish, for not all courses are benevolent roads.

Listen and hear.
See and feel.
Sense and analyze.

For I say to you, if you are not mindful of where your footfalls land, and if you heed not the many omens that rise up before you, then do you foolishly close your eyes to tread a trail darkly.

Consciousness is the ultimate
virtual passageway to everywhere.

*Individuality and its uniqueness
cannot be imitated.*

Within everyone's beingness
lies dormant greatness.

One's Purpose is like a Mist
which envelops self rather than
a singular Mystical Pond one must discover.

Their twinkle of mischief brings laughter.
Their film of tears stirs sorrow.
Their depth of emotion, love.
Oh, those Elf Eyes!
How I love looking into
those magical Elfin Eyes.

Cherish not the leaf, but rather
look to the root and nourish same.
Let not the blossom's beauty be your nectar,
For the seen blossom does wilt and die
While the unseen root lives on.

The people finally did see
that all the Without Trails circled around
and back to that which was
the Beginning . . . the Within Path.
And there they found their Truth.

Above . . . Below . . . Within . . .
the living Soul is made manifest
throughout all dimensional frequencies.

Such is the Spirit's great heritage.

Such is its magnificent vitality
and quintessential beauty of being.

Nature

It can cause your Spirit to soar and
fill your Heart with an overflow of Love
that cannot help but to burst forth in
cascading courses of unbounded emotion—
or it can cause the Spirit to suddenly
plummet in a free-fall and stab your
Heart with sharp pinpricks of
deep empathy.

Nature.
Ever Gentle and Innocent.
Ever Fierce and Wild.
Ever balanced.

To society's perspective there are many Spiritual Philosophies.
To my way of living there is but one.

Spiritual Philosophy is *living* in a manner through which one's *Spirit* is given full consciousness . . . where the *Spirit* is given full freedom to come to the fore to live the experience of life instead of the ego.

Live. Set the *Spirit* free to *live* this life.

The Divine Feminine Aspect is
Friend, Mother, and Lover to all.

The Knowing cannot be made
subjective nor selective.
Most importantly, The Knowing Within
cannot be Silenced.

Attend to your principles
        lest they be allowed to
vacillate like the
        mutable cloud formations
    sent adrift on the whim
        of every breath of breeze.

Visitors to my cabin note the many representations of fairies that are about the place; some sitting on window ledges with stained glass wings, some framed prints on the walls, others are figurines crafted of crystal. When asked what my fascination is with these Little Beings I have no reply other than to say, "My enchantment with them comes not from them being an enigma, but from the fact that they *aren't*."

I am so minuscule.
I am but a mote of dust in the
vast expanse of the Breathing Universe.
Just a speck.
No one.
Only a single heartbeat in
the grand measure of Time.

There are days when the extent and depth of hatred I observe within this world overwhelms my Soul.

These days bring to me the great mystery of how I came to still be here to view the following morn's bright sunrise.

Something primal within me compels me forward through time, each moonrise being the sacred vessel safely transporting me over the dark waters to the receiving shore of dawn.

When one spends a great deal of time out in the deep woods, in the wild old-growth forests, and along the sun-dappled mossy stream banks, one loses the perception of a separate identity as her heartbeat begins to drum in time with Nature's own thundering rhythm. There is no human I anymore, only the beautiful and intensely sensual *feel* of being one singular Primal Cell among the All—senses so full to bursting, so unaffected and real . . . Feral.

There is no sweeter sound to the ear
than the crisp and clear Evensong
echoing through
a deep wood
in twilight.

The winds of Love no longer gust upon me
with a self-absorbed ego and violent force.

The winds of Love now come as a selfless,
gentle spring breeze leaving behind its
sweet fragrance after softly
brushing my cheek with its tender kiss.

True living is dying to Self.
Only then can we behave
in a purely unconditional manner.

Some have said that I'm outspoken, that some of my spiritual philosophies rasp gratingly against the grain of long-held religious tradition. And I would agree. I would say the same of anyone who stands up alone or in a crowd to point at the Emperor and, with conviction, announce the truth, "He has no clothes on!"

Popular belief is not a criteria for Truth. Many times Truth stands alone . . . apart from the crowd. Crowd mentality is not the air which sustains Truth.

Racism and sexism,
homophobia, religious arrogance,
persecution of all diversity.

Oh God, how oft there have been nights when
I've cried myself to sleep over
the hatred I see poisoning
the human minds of this world!

The Ones-Who-Know end up being intended
victims of Those-Who-Don't-Know.
These last are known by their names—
skepticism, denouncement, ridicule,
prejudice, envy, and hatred.

There are those who are skeptics.
There are those who are doubters.
And there are those who prefer to don rose-
colored glasses. To these ones, I have no words;
for they have made their choice, though the signs
have been many.

Yet there are those who wonder. There are
those who have gentle stirrings. And there are
those who have stepped upon the beautiful
Threshold of Awareness—all on the verge of
perceiving That Which Is There To See. To
these ones I say, open your exquisite senses.
Look with fine clarity into That Which Is
Beyond and Beneath, Within and Without.
In these coming critical times, listen to and heed
the directives of your Spirits that retain the high
wisdom you are just now perceiving.

Acceptance shows intelligence and wisdom.
Revenge shows great stupidity and ignorance.

Looking for and thinking you've found mystery in everything perceived will only lead to the disappointment of reality when it hits.

The Great Web of Life is the Grand Cohesion that maintains all living aspects of the Universe as a coalesced Living Unit.

An overscrupulous conscience is corrected by a simple mental adjustment in Philosophy—understanding that you have the right to be the unique individual that you are and the right to express that Uniqueness.

Understanding more of Life
with crystal clarity comes
with having The Knowing
and that wondrous gift is more treasured
and precious than the Hope Diamond.

Our planet cannot survive
if intolerance and hatred do.

Growing toward the Divine means that we increase our behavioral and spiritual philosophical attitudes to a raised level that more closely aligns with all aspects of spiritual goodness.

Growing toward the Divine means to rid Self of ego and all negative behavior, to practice unconditional goodness at every available opportunity.

Dominance has no place in a friendship.

Having Acceptance is having
a very special aspect of grace
laced within one's personal
perspective and philosophy.

Criticizing the appearance of others, whether it be physical shape, color of skin, demeanor, perception of social status, type of clothing, or whatever, indicates an ignorant mind, one full of the perceived perfections of Self as compared to those of others.

Acceptance does not equate to apathy.

Memories can be
the greatest treasure we have.
I wonder why more people
don't recognize that?

What will prove to be humanity's
most valuable asset for the future
will be the ability
to persevere through Acceptance,
to energetically rally
with enthusiasm in the face
of opposition and adversity.

All wars are caused by the ego.

Making wild assumptions
and endless speculation
over the causes for some events is fruitless.

The esoteric, the mysterious,
miracles of religion
all overshadow the intellect of reality.

If you live a life of unconditional goodness,
you've probably already fulfilled
your Purpose for being here.

The spiritual quality of being childlike is
not the same as behavioral immaturity.

Denying Reality is an attempt
to create one's own reality.

Release your Child Within and see if
you don't love the new freedom felt.

Reality changes each hour, each minute. We make tentative plans for the future and accept that which alters those plans. By doing this we remain flexible and make alternate adjustments. By doing this we maintain a wonderful fluid state of being that cushions the unforeseen bumps and bruises we receive along the way. Acceptance keeps us supple.

The intellectual and emotional companionship
of a friend has no equal.

Articles of faith do not
take the place of
personal responsibility
and awareness,
nor will they negate destiny.

Sometimes the passing of time
has a clever way of
turning fiction into nonfiction.

Preconceptions are blinding.
Preconceptions close the eyes and ears
for those who cross paths
with the true teacher who subtly
whispers the Sacred Words.

Information and knowledge are good.
They're wonderful.
So is rationale.
But there's something even greater—
    the Wisdom of Foresight.

Life is literally loaded
with spiritual teachers.
They go about unnoticed because
their appearance and demeanor
are colored by people's self-prescribed
designer concept of them which,
in turn, closes the eyes and ears
to their presence.

The Age of the Divine Mother is dawning.
The truth of Her Nature
will light up the world like seven suns.
And the patriarchal religions
will bend their knees in acknowledgement.

Meditation is not a requirement
for gaining spiritual maturity.

There is nothing that can break down
the hard shell covering soft human emotion
and attitudes more than a mother's love.

The Divine does not favor
an intricately worded traditional prayer
over one that comes spontaneously
from one's own heart.

Consciousness is
the intelligent energy of the Spirit.

Spiritual maturity is thought and behavior
that reflects the Light
of the Trinity's Divine Aspects.

Consciousness is the Eternal Life within us.
Consciousness is the individual's Eternal Mind.

The Knowing is recognized by its clarity and simplicity, which is so beautiful that there are no words to write them down with, no images to verbalize to another.

The Knowing comes as bright bursts of inspiration, heart-thumping epiphanies, and waves of warm emotion. It comes not as words, but as a sudden vision, a clear vision displaying Reality in all its magnificent majesty.

A Spiritual Gift is not truly spiritual
if *anything* is expected in return
for its sharing with others.

Spiritual development is derived
from the expansion and blend
of the intellectual and behavioral facets
of Self. The behavioral aspect
is that which reflects
the spiritual development of the intellect.

Life transgressions can be balanced
in any dimension, in any
vibrational frequency of existence.

The Knowing transcends the Ego,
and the Self is suddenly—
nowhere to be found.

If you're searching for spiritual knowledge
and truths, you have to look
to the Spirit of Self rather than
within the material world.

Unless one reaches the stage of recognizing the confinements of conceptualized book learning and understands that so much more depth of knowledge lies *beyond* its limitations, that individual's mind will forever remain in a spiritually undeveloped state, where behavior is likewise reflected through evidence of the Ego holding sway.

The individual who gives of oneself
in a completely selfless manner
is exhibiting greatness.
The individual who practices
Unconditional Goodness is actively
carrying out her purpose in life.
Make your *entire* life your purpose
rather than throwing away
valuable time looking for it.

The more one reads and contemplates that which has been studied, the more one realizes that traditional knowledge is rigid with molded concepts. The more concepts one comes to recognize, the more one feels boxed in by them. The more one is boxed in, the greater the urge to break free of the traditional knowledge that binds and to reach into the Beyond, which beckons with the bright promise of rich refinements of knowledge that come not as unyielding concepts, but as a gentle and sure Knowing.

True greatness is often overlooked
in favor of an overblown perception
of what a true accomplishment is.

Everyone we've ever been
has blended to create the Totality
of each individual Spirit.

It is the human Ego that turns the simplicity of purpose into complexity. The Ego refuses to believe a purpose can be as simple as being a good person, but rather is of the false opinion that one needs to attain some type of self-perceived greatness in life.

Book learning provides us with a jumping-off point from the linear to the nonlinear, from form to formless, from the known to the possible. It leads us along the fence lines of traditional conceptual confinements to the gate that is marked with the words: There Is More Through Here. And it is at this point when we leave the rigid concepts of traditional knowledge behind and pass through the gateway to greater understanding.

Meditation is great, but it is not *the* great conduit to the Divine Minds in lieu of the many other methods available for gaining quietude.

Everything has its price.

Watch what you bring to the table.

Life is full of two-edged swords.

Many actions exact a payment of high interest.

All pipers demand to be paid.

The way to the Divine is through
spiritual behavior
rather than
religious beliefs.

No marriage or loving partnership can be a synergistically based one if one individual within said relationship claims superiority over the other and expects deference in all things.

Scripture is loaded with assumptions
and false rationales
devised to *fix* inconsistencies.

Ego causes the chaos.

There are no senior partners in a marriage.
If Love is real, each marriage partner
will respect and honor the other's
individuality, talents, and inherent rights.

A parent's most valuable
gifts to a child are . . .
Unconditional Love and Acceptance.

Only someone *fearful* of another individual threatening to injure their ego will attempt to keep others down (suppressed) in a position perceived as being *below* that of Self.

The greatest threat to untruth . . . is Truth.
The greatest proof of Truth . . . is Time.
Truth cannot be threatened nor can it be
intimidated . . . nor killed.

We, as the children of the divine, were meant to be finely tuned with our balance brought into a precisely calibrated state of being.

Seeing human perfection is a hallucination.
Believing in human perfection is a delusion.

A truly spiritual society is one that is
neither patriarchal nor matriarchal.

You never have to concern yourself
with the "why of your karma"
if you just remember—In life, do no harm.

The Divine Minds are displeased
with negative behavior,
not with people.

Will is the Prime Factor
in spiritual development.
It's through the strength of Will
and its choices in life that all
negative factors can be ultimately conquered.

Today we've ended up with a multitude of concepts that have shed (buried) their feminine Deity origination. The Goddesses have been conveniently erased from societal memory and, therefore, it is generally assumed that they must've been imaginary characters of fable, myth, and legend.

Ethnic egotism will be a perspective
that will not survive in our future world.

When looking for a scapegoat to blame,
we do others great harm; consequently,
we do ourselves greater harm in the process.
Searching for one to blame is
not being in Acceptance of What Is.

Nobody is born a perversion.
The Divine never created
a perverted being . . . ever.

Angelic Beings have no physical form.
Angelic Beings are of Light.
They are of Pure Thought.

The Spiritual Forces help those
who first try to help themselves.

The Dark Force within society that has grown into such a cannibalistic monster is none other than Ego with a capital E.

Mystical experiences are meaningless in and of themselves unless the individual has assimilated them in a developmental manner and has come away with an understanding and behavioral appreciation of their attending Wisdom.

Self-Righteousness is egotistical arrogance often twisted like putty and made into something that's supposed to resemble a pleasing gift to God.

Methods of physical self-protection do not equate to being in fear or having a lack of faith, It's being smart enough to be Prepared and have Self-Reliance.

Pure Mind is a wonder to behold.

Spiritual pursuit is wonderful,
but not when one turns one's back
on another for its attainment.

Biblical times didn't possess a monopoly on Angelic manifestations nor the possibility of people having spiritual intuitiveness and the experience of visions.

Prayer is free expression
of the heart, mind, and soul.

The Trinity's compassion
is unbounded and has no limits.

One can choose to make moments of prayer, or one can make Life an eternal prayer that never reaches the amen stage until the last breath is exhaled.

Intuitive spirituality exists for everyone. It lives everywhere because it comes from the Universal Mind of the Divine Aspects.

Having the wisdom to recognize an inevitability is not the same as having a fatalistic worldview.

Epiphanies that come as heart-welling explosions of wisdom and spiritual light change one forever. You are never the same again.

The important aspects of life become clear only after the former priorities have proven to be shallow and destructive. There will come a time when the true spiritual priorities stand out like a diamond gleaming among the coals.

Living in the physical
with a mind to the Spiritual Light
is how we evolve back into the Light.

The crisp delineation and separatism of the different religions will dull as it blends into a more unified, conceptual spiritual ideology.

All of Life is sacred.
All that has been Divinely created is sacred.

The Here and Now
is our beautiful chance
to make it all happen.

A friend of mine made an interesting observation about people's various perceptions of me. He said, "You gift people with a beautiful, symmetrical sculpture. Some people just observe its beauty and come away with a sense of fulfillment for having been exposed to its essence; some people take it as a possession and build an altar around it; and others melt it down into some misshapen form and claim that *that* was your grotesque gift to humankind."

I think my friend was not only extremely perceptive, but also very accurate in his observation of people's view of me. Some see simple Truth and are touched, some see an imagined Deity and feel the need to elevate, and some twist and deform reality with hatred. Yet all the while, regardless of people's perception of me, I remain the same . . . just me.

Don't ever let anyone tell you what you
should or shouldn't read or listen to.
This is giving away your
power to choose for Self
what you believe.

Understanding the technicalities of consciousness and its vast potentialities does not become a prerequisite to experiencing those realities or even having the basic *acknowledgement* of them.

Life is watching bad things happen to good people and good things happen to bad people. Rhyme or reason are haphazard. Trying to figure it out can spin one in dizzying circles. The spinning finally stops when Acceptance comes into one's heart.

Our little Third Dimension is so minuscule, so fragmentary contrasted to the massive Whole of Reality. There are literally worlds—Universes—out there just existing and ready for our consciousness to discover and interact within.

The Dark Forces are the greed, hatred, jealousy, prejudice, racism, sexism, vindictiveness, and egotistical negatives.

These darknesses in people are powerful forces manifesting evil behavior poisoning our world.

Reality awaits the untethered consciousness.

Until it is fully explored, for some, reality—the only reality recognized as real—will remain bound to the simple confinements of the Third Dimension.

If there were such a place as Hell, it would be right here where all the tormented and vile humans hide their gruesome selves behind a smiling mask and cover their true stench with cologne.

Though we don't always understand the workings of reality, it exists just the same. It exists in spite of our mind's incomprehension.

The Book of Revelation was a dream.
And dreams are symbolism.

The alignment of perspective with Reality should be everyone's priority if they have any interest in recognizing Truth.

Psychic abilities do not define
a spiritually aware or highly developed
spiritual state of being.

Internalizing the negativity of another
opens Self to same.
It gives permission to enter without resistance.

A perceptive mind recognizes negativity when exhibited in others and does not internalize it.

Spiritual concepts are nothing
without the spiritual human behavior
to put them into action.

Relativity frequently plays a vital role when deriving an ultimate solution or answer to any philosophical inquiry.

Love, Unconditional Goodness, and Selflessness are priceless jewels we are all blessed with possessing. They are part of the treasure of natural riches we all have. Whether we choose to share or hoard those riches is up to each of us. It's a personal, conscious choice, our behavior. A personal choice.

Not realizing your own personal power shifts that power to others, who will then use it through their own control mechanisms.

Human perfection is a contradiction in terms.

—Introspection—

The way to understanding.

The way to knowing self.

Control by others is born
through the victim's permission of it
and is sustained through submission.
Control, psychic or psychological,
cannot survive in a state
of resistance or neutrality.
Control exists only when it is *allowed* to.

One facet of the spectacular Spirit Crystal Within represents but a singular fragment of the Who of you. One unique experience does not make a total individual or Spirit. One unique experience *adds* color and dimension to enhance the ongoing formation of one's composite spirit essence.

Karma is not
the catchall answer
to everything that
happens in one's life.

Prayer is a way of life.
Prayer is living goodness.
In this manner are we fulfilling our
spiritual Potential on a daily basis.
In this Manner are we the magnificent
Living Lights the Divine Source
envisioned us to Be.

Phrase prayers to represent
an understanding of destiny
rather than your own will.

Why do people think
righteousness is subjective . . .
to their own personal interpretation?

Grandmother Earth,

the wise Old Woman of the Woods,

the Greatest Teacher of all.

At every turn Her Wisdom

is freely gifted to us

as an offering of Unconditional Love,

but only if we have the eyes to see,

the ears to hear,

the mind to perceive,

and the heart to receive.

Walk softly through life.

Attend to the placement of each footfall lest you unintentionally cause Grandmother Earth pain or disrupt the smooth and soothing rhythm of her beating pulse.

The key to motion is Light
combined with understanding
the fluid interfacing
of gravity and magnetic fields.

Twilight—the magical time when
the doors to a woman's
three houses are opened wide.

Every job well done is an achievement.
That is the Divine's
perspective on accomplishment.
That is the Divine's view
of an individual's self-worth.

The Evening Star
becomes the Morning Star
and that's why there is the . . . Blue Star.

The Wiser the woman,
the simpler her joys
and the greater her blessings.
For, in truth, her clear eyes see only
Reality's pure quality of true value.

The Cosmos sings in sacred chant
to the Divine Sophia.
The stars shimmer with Her reflected glory.
And Her precious breath is the Gift of Life
That moves the Universe in ordered symmetry.

Love is Spirit's drawn breath.

I am far from being above a single Soul
upon this earthly ground,
for the wisdom I share has come
at great cost—by way
of living life's tribulations
and sorrows of the human heart.
Oh no, I am far from being above
because the greatest Wisdom gained
comes only from being among.

Sometimes the Light isn't seen
until a life is given for it.

Psalm to Sophia
(for protection)

Lead my cause, sweet Sophia, with those who would walk with me, hold back those who would fight against me.

2. Take thy shield and sword and stand up for mine aid.

3. Hold up thy spear and bar the way against those who would persecute me, and say unto my receiving soul, I am thy companion.

4. Let them be foiled and put to shame those who seek to destroy the integrity of your message, let them be turned back and brought to confusion those who devise my hurt or rejoice in wounding the heart.

5. Let them be as willowed chaff before the wind and let your avenging angel swiftly carry them off on the wind.

6. Let their way be tangled in their own discontent and let your angels chastise them for their erring ways.

7. For without cause hath they tried to find fault with me and hath twisted my words into snares of their own making.

8. Let barriers come upon them at unawares, and let their twisted net that they hath devised catch only themselves.

9. And my soul shall be joyous in Sophia's Divine Light.

10. False witnesses did rise up and they laid to my charge many things that I knew not about.

11. Still I behaved as though they were my sister, my brother, but in mine adversity did they rejoice and gather themselves together against me with jealousy and hatred held as precious jewels to their breasts.

12. With hypocritical mockers in feasts they gnashed upon me with their teeth.

13. Oh, Sweet Sophia, abide within me and be my eternal Guard against those ones who do not hear nor see with the soul's simple clarity.

14. I will give thee thanks and I will praise thee all my days until I am old and exhale my last breath.

15. Let not those who call themselves mine enemies wrongfully rejoice over me, neither let them cast aspersions those who hate without cause.

16. For they speak not of peace and love, but they devise deceitful matters against all those who walk quietly upon the land.

17. Sweet Sophia, be never far from me.

18. Stir thyself and attend with compassion to our cause.

19. See me, Sweet One, according to thine ordained plan and let the ignorant ones not rejoice over us.

20. Let them be ashamed after seeing their wrongdoing and open their eyes to thine light and unseal their ears to thine words.

21. And my soul shall speak of thine beauty and magnify thine splendor all the remaining days of my life.

The Eyes are beautiful Gifts
yet there are more things that
are unseen than are visible.

It's not the guns killing people,
It's hatred pulling the triggers.

The quality of Humility is not pure if it's contaminated by a thirst for recognition.

Crop Circles . . . most made
by playful humans.

Oh, how I love Autumn!

When the days of Fall are so deliciously delictable I lie out in the woods and become an absolute glutton while I ravenously drink in the sunshine nectar, voraciously eat of Nature's sweetness, and bask in the fragrantly soothing breeze as it sensuously massages this old tired body and touches the chimes of the quaking aspen leaves to bring tranquil music to this poor Soul in need of deep serenity.

In bygone days, those of yore,
I was so full of roaring fire.
Embers now,
Glowing softly,
Restrain the blaze
To a single flame.

The great nothing
unbidden
comes upon me
and blankets
my Soul
with
Time's black shroud.

This date is September 21, 1999 and
every cell in this body is trembling
with exquisite joy, for the high alpine
air is caressing my hair and the warming
brilliance of the sun is kissing my cheek.
What a glorious blessing to walk among the
golden and amber aspens as they chime their
quaking leaves and bring music to these
receiving ears. My heart sings out a sacred
chant to the sweet Goddess Who breathed
such precious life into Nature's beingness and
my Soul whispers prayers of thanksgiving
for all that I've been gifted with witnessing.

When I pass from this world
I shall call upon my Spirit
to manifest all my days as
mirror images
of this one
I now walk through.

The one element about the people of this beautiful Earth that I found most difficult to live with was their verbal and physical cruelty to one another. I never came to a clear understanding behind why they found these so necessary. And they never came to a clear understanding of why they were compelled to hurt others in such spiteful and mean-spirited ways. People just do not realize the pain they inflict with their thoughtless words and deeds.

If you haven't pinned down
your Purpose for being here,
you can start with living the Vow
your Spirit made just prior to entry
into this physical realm—
"First, Do No Harm."
Where do you think the author
of the Hippocratic Oath got that from?

The purest hearts I ever came across
while living on this planet
were beating within the little ribcages
of my loving and faithful dogs.
Never did they have an agenda—
other than Love.

I've never had another agenda in life
other than trying to make a difference,
trying to bring greater spirituality to
the masses, and sharing what Truths
I've come to know.
I've always tried to be a good person,
yet persecution
shadowed all of my days.

Solitude within the autumn woods.
Deep blue sky,
Brilliant orange aspens,
sunlight streaming through high pines,
union with the Divine.

Some folks have said
that "I've no life outside my books."
Yet this statement only shows
how ignorant of me they are,
for those who do know me well
also know that my books were
always and ever a minuscule
fragment of my daily life—
of my beingness and work.

Though I cautioned them to not
try to identify the Goddess,
they made
wild assumptions
and
false accusations
anyway.

Seeing with the Eye,
Hearing with the Ear,
Brings hard information to mind.

Seeing and hearing
With the Soul
Brings gentle wisdom to mind.

The Eye and the Ear
Are not enough.

Only by perceiving
Through the Soul
Is the Spirit of Reality understood.

Some nights a deep heartache awakens me, and I am forced to pace the cabin until it subsides. But it never really completely goes away, for the heartache is a soulache for the skeptics.

While you spent your days
looking for them in human form,
voluntarily did you choose
to miss the Sophia and Shekinah
when they passed before your eyes—
for They are of Pure Spirit.

I have been hated.

I have been loved.

To those who've hated I give you joy
in knowing my writing is nearly done.
To those who've loved I give you joy
in knowing that, by holding this book,
you hold my heart.

The myriad ways I witnessed my words being twisted scorched my heart and nearly cut short my writings. Yet what turned the tide were those who listened and gave soothing balm to the burns that healed the heart and uplifted my resolve above the mire to continue on and write it all until the last word was penned. Without realizing it, all the brilliantly shining, aware Souls of this world became the Living Lights who championed my cause and chased away the effects of the Living Shadows who attempted to thwart my purpose.

To all those powerful Living Lights—

You know who you are—

I'm deeply grateful.

You are, each one of you,

among the precious blessings I count each day.

If, in your future,
   you should happen to recall
      an author named Summer Rain,
         remember her as someone who cared—
            remember her as nothing more than that.
Caring.
   Breathing life back into the idea of Love.
      Reminding people to stop hating each other.
         That's enough to remember.
            That's all that's important.

The Divine lives within the
pulsating DNA of the All.

Allowing one's maturing child the
freedom of independent thinking
is one of the
greatest Gifts of Love
a parent can bless a child with.

Silence is the most profound sound.

For society to advance, we must live life through the Spirit rather than through the Ego. It's the Ego that distorts our perception and skews the true meaning and value of beauty and power.

Many times, the problem with seeking
is in the seeking.

True Beauty is Spirit deep.

No one is an only child, for we are all siblings in the Family of Humankind.

Envy denies free expression of Self and smothers Acceptance. It germinates the dark seeds of hatred and animosity. It has the capability of growing into a clinging vine that chokes individuality and darkening our worldview with shadowed and convoluted perspectives.

To be content with the status quo is to be mentally satisfied with an ongoing state of voluntary stagnation where intellectual growth is forever stunted and new thought becomes a taboo.

Here's one to ponder—

Can the practice of constant Unconditional Goodness become a flaw in one's life, in one's character?

There is no "American Dream."
Only the dreams of human beings.
For it is only the "Human Dream"
That recognizes possibilities.

Isn't it amazing that, sometimes, the innocence of one's loving pet can be the only grounding element on days when it seems the whole world's gone crazy?

There're several scary aspects about human behavior. One is that, frequently, majority opinion or belief can completely eradicate the clear and obvious facts of reality. One such example was ignoring the true and actual date of the millennium just because the majority wanted to celebrate it when the New Year turned to 2000.

Love gives life its strongest heartbeat.

Aren't the "Right to Life" folks committing the very act they claim a sin when they bomb clinics and shoot doctors?

There is no "Mother of God."
Unless, of course, you're talking
about Sophia, the Creatrix,
Who was born of the Primal Silence.

I'm nothing, nothing at all.
Only the word is something.
I'm nothing. Not even a voice.
Except, perhaps,
a simple amplifier for the voice.

Is the Universe oblivious to the events
happening in one, single, human's Life?
Never!

A Life goal—or purpose—can be as simple as striving toward never letting one's heart be numbed or forever deadened to empathy.

Eights upon eights

Double Helix

DNA strands

Silken threads to the Web of Life.

Pure as newfallen snow in blue alpine moonlight is the day before you at the appearance of each new dawn.

A springtime walk in the woods fills my senses. Wafting up from the sweet Earth was an intoxicating fertile fragrance that brought strong impressions of a verdant Life Force full of rich nourishment that I likened to the Earth Mother's pulsating umbilical—throbbing . . . throbbing with enough engorged nutrients to sustain all of Nature's thirsting needs. The scent, the scent so readily associated with her womanly fragrance of pungent fertility.

In the man-made world of asphalt and cement,
there is a serene Garden of Tranquility
that one can carry Within—
always there—always Within.

People build prison bars around themselves
with iron perceptions and then
are forced to see the world
through the narrow spaces
of their own limited viewpoints.

My purpose was not to make philosophical waves nor even a visible spiritual ripple. But rather to strengthen the quiet and unseen current of truth silently moving beneath them. A current that is full of timelessness.

Intelligence is as a pretty woman.
She has no lasting charm
or natural, quiet grace
without Wisdom.

Our galaxy is called the Milky Way.
There are a hundred billion *other* galaxies.
Our galaxy is but a single grain
of sand in the Universe.
Earth—one molecular cell
of that singular grain.

Carbon dioxide emissions from Earth erode away the protective layer of ozone surrounding our precious planet.

Depletion of our atmospheric ozone creates a destructive and powerfully long-lasting Greenhouse Effect.

The Greenhouse Effect will create a global warming so pervasively dramatic and reach a magnitude so unprecedented that it will eventually inundate all continental coastal and inland waterway cities with rising levels of ocean, lake, and river waters that will flood or submerge them all.

Most industries aren't doing anything about it.

OPEC sits on its growing profits.

Governments don't push fossil fuel laws through.

But You can make a difference!

Decidious trees *absorb* carbon dioxide from our fragile atmosphere.

Help our Mother Earth.

Plant a tree . . . a *leafy* tree.

Plant two or three!

Let not the glitter of glory be your impetus for goodness, but rather the quiet shine that glows from the Heart Within. Acts of goodness are not goodness if glory is a goal.

It is possible to physically exist
in two different centuries simultaneously.
Ah, Reality, what a riddle you can be.
What a joy to discover and behold.

More weighty than a bar of gold,
an Oscar, Emmy, or any gilded plaque,
is a basketful of goodness.

Knock and it shall be opened to you.
Are you knocking on the right door?
The door leading to the Within?

When Life becomes Unpredictable and the Ground one stands upon turns Unstable, there is a Consistency in Nature that can be depended on to return that precious Grounding Force to one's Perspective that Balances the Equilibrium of all Rationale.

Nature needs not mechanical clocks
   nor see the turn of an hourglass
   to mark an hour's passing.
For the turn of Her Face
   and the Trail of Her Journey
   is, Herself, the created Timepiece
   of Gaia.

Too oft we perceive ourselves
as composed of skin and bones,
hair and organs, yet rarely
do we look beyond our gross anatomy
to the finer facets of same, for within us
is a shimmering Cosmos
undulating with the Pulse of Life.

I look upon the sun-dappled forest floor
and spy traces of footfalls
that have passed this way before me.
Deep in the woods, I hear the screech
of a single owl; behind me,
rustling in the brush gives evidence that
I am not alone—ever.
Burnt-orange kinnikinnick leaves
touched with red, a glint of mica
winking up at me along the trail,
the sudden flight of a hidden quail—
all my relations.
And a smile bursts forth from my heart.

A spiritual Truth can only be a controversy
when presented before a false belief,
when set down beside an Untruth.

True Beauty has no enemies.
Yet True Beauty is enhanced by
two things—Time and Wisdom.

Rumors can
  Sear a heart
  Ruin a reputation
  Kill a love.
Rumors can be Deadly.

The Seven Deadly Sins

Hatred

Gossip

Egotism

Infidelity

Intolerance

Spiritual Arrogance

Conditional Goodness

Acceptance is not the surrender
of free will or one's faith.
Acceptance is never equated to apathy.

Personal Belief never negates the fact that everyone's life holds promise.

Life is not about winning or losing
because Life is not a game.

Upon a glittering blanket of crystal
diamonds touched by blue moonlight,
Among the intoxicating fragrance
of a profusion of meadow wildflowers,
Beneath a canopy of midsummer green
in the sun-dappled forest,
Beside a singing stream
on a carpet of soft moss,
On a newfallen quilt of autumn leaves,
In the sparkle of morning dew,
In the gold of alpenglow,
And magic of twilight,
Everywhere,
I love to love you.

I know some Sillies.

The Sillies think they're smart.

They think Wisdom is the same thing
as knowledge.

They think Wisdom is identical to intelligence.

Nay, I say.

Though people can spend a lifetime reading and
learning, though they be born with a Mensa
level intelligence quotient, Wisdom will not be
theirs until it has slowly and, with gentleness,
grown quietly forth from deep within themselves.

Unconditional Love isn't hard to come by.
Unconditional Love isn't hard to have,
hold, and express from the Heart
once one has, holds, and expresses
Acceptance within the Mind.

So you think your life is the pitts?

So you think there's nothing to be happy
about or grateful for?

Every thing in your life that isn't broken
is a blessing.

Every situation or relationship that isn't
problematical is a blessing.

Everything in your life that's not a negative has to be something else.

What is that something else?

Could it be a positive that can be perceived
as a blessing?

Think about that.

Really think about it.

Soft as down.

Lusciously fragrant with sweet
fertileness.

The mossy bank,

Soft as silk.

With closed eyes,

And wide opened Heart,

I surrender.

I would not cover you in cold jewels.
I would not wrap you with the world.
I would not smother you with empty dreams.
I would shelter you with true friendship.
I would bundle you in abandoned joy.
I would cloak you in sweet orchids.

The Wise One never speaks of impossibilities,
For She knows well the Wisdom
of their ultimate improbabilites.

An open mind is forever awed
by the spectacular visions
of Reality's fathomless depths,
While the closed mind continually stagnates
in the imprisoned cell of moldy thought.

Visible beauty is only
as lovely as inner beauty does.

Everlasting is the journey of those seeking only friends blessed with fair weather.

A shadow can be touched

    yet never carried about in one's hand.

A sunbeam can be walked through

    yet never boxed for a gift.

Alpenglow can be seen

    yet cannot be captured in a bottle.

Our world is full of realities

    that are not three-dimensional.

So too are the worlds of quantum meditation.

Intolerance is a
dark societal menace
bringing a pandemic
of
spiritual paralysis
to
humanity.

The more separatist terms society makes for itself, the farther apart the members of the Human Family drift.

Instead of allowing our differences to consume us with the fire of intolerance, we must recognize and embrace the many commonalities that bind us.

Whenever I happen to overhear vicious slander
I respect one's precious right to free speech and
grieve over how that sacred right has been so
wantonly desecrated with foul intent.

Sooner or later . . .
improbability becomes
the mother of inevitability.

People spend entire lifetimes
diligently searching for the answers to
age-old mysteries that will only prove
to sustain their subtle enigmatic conundrums
until . . . the right questions are asked.

The Thirty-Six.
Just thirty-six people with Pure Hearts
keep this world from ending.
Just thirty-six.

Starlight makes me giggle.
Sunshine melts away cares.
Moonbeams lift me home.

It has been said that
"You can't take it with you when you die."
They're wrong.
You can take something . . . Love.

"Mirror, Mirror, on the wall, why was I born?"

"You chose to be."

"Mirror, Mirror, on the wall, why did I choose to be born?"

"To accomplish a purpose."

"Mirror, Mirror, on the wall, what's my purpose?"

"To make a difference."

"Mirror, Mirror, on the wall, what kind of difference?"

"A positive one."

"Mirror, Mirror, on the wall, which positive one?"

"That's another choice."

"Mirror, Mirror, on the wall, will it be an earth-shattering choice?"

"Don't kid yourself. Dreams of fame come from tiny minds. Stop thinking so small. These choices silently slip into your life like clockwork . . . expect them to appear tomorrow, in the next hour, the next moment. Like the visible movement of a clock's swinging pendulum, the choices tick toward you in a syncopated pattern of opportunity. They are the rhythms of one's life. They are the repeated refrains of one's chosen destiny."

"Mirror, Mirror, on the wall, how do I hear these refrains?"

"By listening."

"Mirror, Mirror, on the wall, how do I know the ticking is for me?"

"By listening to your heart."

"Mirror, Mirror, on the wall, what if I don't want to act on every opportunity that comes within the pattern of my destiny?"

"Ahh, and so it is that you've so quickly forgotten why you were born."

Wear Love not as a garment that
can be changed according to one's mood.
Wear love as a second skin that
becomes the living cellular structure
of your core Beingness.

The "Dead of Winter" is a misnomer.
It's a contradiction in terms,
for winter is
the beautiful season of transitions
when hope and the anticipation of renewals
beat strong within the human heart.

Have a respectful
measure of honor
regarding your
ethnicity and spiritual beliefs,
yet never harbor the
arrogance of superiority
for these
within the heart.

All of Reality must be a miracle
because the unknowns of physics
that are still veiled from human discovery
are termed: "Miracles."

What ignorance chooses to call a miracle,
intellectual discovery ends up calling Reality.

Twilight is a silent conjuress.
Recognize and respect her attributes
and She'll hand you the key
to Reality's dimensional door,
where the threshold of Consciousness
is but one step away.

Tolerance and Acceptance
of
one another's individuality
is a
spiritual imperative.

Truth makes no bargains.

All that is seen with the eye is not necessarily
that which the mind interprets it as being.
A mirage, though seen, is still an illusion.
And that illusion is a viable element of reality.

Acceptance is not the same
as resentful resignation.

Some religious beliefs create such a destructive force within the congregational body they're as a malignancy metastasizing throughout society.

These beliefs are like a fatal virus riding the insidious vector of the faithful's zealousness as each member at a meeting revels in the joyful complicity of reinforcing each other's contagion.

What the consciousness experiences on any one of the many dimensional levels of Reality is just as real as those events it experiences in the weighty third-dimensional plane.

The season of winter
is none other than poised potential.

Be wary of those
who would attempt
to woo you into a belief
that humans are Divine.

The season of winter is likened to
the grand passageway of Life.
A Corridor of Transition
where one makes an *entry* into the
passageway whenever certain situations
in life come to an *ending*.
And, moving through the Corridor,
exits into the brilliant sunlight
of a new beginning.
Life's situational endings are
the Corridor's entry door.
The Corridor's exit door
leads to new beginnings.
One may pass through many
winter seasons in one year.

I once was a silly old woman who thought her heart was so full of Love that it couldn't hold anymore . . . until I held my grandbaby.

There is a heady fragrance that I love best,
Yet It's so rare that
It only releases its potent scent
but once a year.
It arrives on the whispers of the wind
And is so powerful that it fills the senses
so completely that it's not detected
again for another year.
Autumn.
The arrival of autumn in the air.

Imagination is the powerful
catalyst for discovery.

Throughout life, sometimes we may have to
endure impoverished financial situations, yet
never should we ever have to endure
an emotional impoverishment of the heart.

Acceptance and Tolerance are two
of the Seven Sacred Keys.

More than striving to be a "'Man's Man" or a "Woman's Woman," reach for the glorious goal of being a "Human's Human"—the quintessential Spiritual Being.

There's nothing more awesomely stunning than the potent power of Quiet Wisdom.

The most alluring attributes
a human can have are
gentleness
and a fearless expression of
emotional sensitivity.

Life's possibilities are those priceless gems
that glitter with untold facets of probabilities.

The Human Life has rhythm and meter, each person's identifiable song being unique and dramatically distinct. And every variation within that metered rhythm represents some type of alteration made in the flow of the individual's recognized norm.

Loyalty will not tolerate adoration.
Loyalty must stand alone.
And it does.

If you're fortunate enough to have been born
with a special skill,

    freely share it . . . unconditionally.

If you've been blessed with having a gift of
healing or insight,

    freely share it . . . unconditionally.

May Unconditional Love be your sword,
And may quiet Wisdom be your shield.

Immaturity is never so sad a sight
as when expressed by an adult.
It is an error to assume
that immaturity is confined to youth.

I was once blessed with observing a magnificent butterfly spread wide its fragile, gossamer wings and fly free of its disgarded chrysalis.

I was once blessed with observing a magnificent Spirit spread wide its fragile, gossamer wings and fly free of its disgarded casing.

I was twice blessed.

Clear vision supplies the reassurance
that replaces the need for hope
caused by the unknown.

Loyalty lacking integrity
is nothing but a disguise.

When examining one's loyalties, if any form of self-serving motivations or secret agendas are found lurking in the shadowy corners, then those loyalties are severely compromising the quality of one's personal integrity.

One's loyalty to others should never be blind.

When tempted to utter an unkind word,
show wisdom . . . choose silence.

Nature blesses my Heart with childlike joy.
The mountains bless my mind
with unending inspiration.
And my Love blesses my entire life,
my Soul, with meaning.

There is no emotion
more manic-depressive than Love.
It can make one soar
to the hightest heights of ecstacy,
And it can make one plunge
into the deepest depths of despair.
Love . . . the only bi-polar emotion.

Never let Love sleep.
If one allows it to even doze off,
it'll awake and never again be the same.

Balance.

The Balance of Life is never exhibited in such an exactingly pure form as it is in Nature.

Nature has no dark side . . .
only a balancing side.

There is little appreciation felt for a rainfall without the long dry spell that preceded it.

A time of personal inner serenity is never more deeply relished than when it comes on the heels of a time of strife and tribulation.

A clear, blue sky is rarely counted as a divine blessing until it seems to miraculously appear after a week of nonstop, torrential rain.

Why?

One of the greatest, enigmatic questions
of all time that people ask themselves is:
Why am I here?
Why this question is even such a mystery
is a separate mystery in itself
because the answer is so simple.
Each and every one of us is here
to make a difference in another's life
and to Love Unconditionally.
Quintessential simplicity.

The greatest societal advances
and scientific discoveries
come not from the human intellect,
but from the limitless
wellspring of visionary imagination.

The man whose nature is inherently gentle
possesses a dynamic, quiet power—
a subtle magnetic appeal.

The terms "Excuse" and "Reason"
are not truly synonymous.
An excuse can carry a tone of prevarication.
A reason rings of credibility.

Releasing one's Child Within
is not the same as relinquishing
one's attained level of maturity.

It's good to frequently peek behind your acts of goodness, for, if reasons be found lurking there, those acts lack the precious quality of being unconditional.

If the reason is to be liked and appreciated, then the acts are never deserving of the appreciation received.

The more resentment you carry around with you, the greater and heavier your baggage load becomes.

True perseverance through life's tribulations precludes having a sense of persecution.

Lady Magdalene, like Sappho,
was an accomplished lyricist, writer,
and an adept leader of women.

There are times when the greatest wisdom
is spoken in the language of silence.

Acquiring one of the keys to serenity is
not in the getting, but in the letting go.

Mother Nature.
I can feel every element of Her as
all Her magical aspects course through
every fiber of my being.
The Old Woman of the Woods is all to me.
She is my mother, sister, companion, mentor,
and the breath of my Soul.

True value is the highest attribute of
the untouchable aspects in life.

When the Self is prioritized above all else,
the true qualities of value
become a highly distorted perception
which cripples one's ability to
effectively relate to Reality in a
productively functional manner.

Zeal that smothers rationale is blind ignorance.

There is no personal gain
if integrity is forfeited for it.

The greatest epiphanies appear
when least expected.
The brightest sparks of wisdom
come unbidden.
The seeker often hampers discovery
with the effort of seeking.

Having a sense of Ego that's stronger than
the mind's intellectual rationale and reason
is likened to being afflicted
with an addiction to self.

Frustration comes from
not having acceptance for what is.
Frustration comes from not wanting to wait
for That Which Will Be.

Self-doubts are often like a shroud
voluntarily wrapped about oneself.

Shadows of doubt
negate the solidity, the surety,
of convictions.

If it's really true that
"To Forgive is Divine,"
then I suppose that's precisely the reason why
we humans find it so difficult to do!

Wisdom is the force within.

Acceptance carries unlimited power.

A brilliant mind becomes mundane

if it outshines the brilliance of one's Soul.

Which type of illumination
bestows greater clarity,
Sunshine or moonlight?

Would you believe in Something that cannot be touched because it has no substance? Something that cannot be approached because it appears to move away from you every time you get nearer? And then vanishes into thin air right before your very eyes?

If you saw this Something, would you deny your experience? Doubt your eyes because you found no rationale to ground it to? Call it an illusion because it appeared illogical to all your knowns? Maybe attribute it to a momentary hallucination due to exhaustion? A perceptual trick of the mind perhaps? Or would your sighting alone be enough to instill confirmed belief?

Such is the stuff Nature is created of. Such is the wondrous stuff Reality is made of. Such is the nature of a rainbow, a ray of sunlight, and so much more.

You'll see.

One day, when it becomes one of those everyday elements of common knowledge, you'll see that events experienced in the Virtual Reality of Quantum Meditation are even more real than those which one currently believes is the *only* reality of the so very simplistic third dimension.

You'll see.

Is Belief based on seeing?
Or is the conviction behind one's belief
based on faith alone?
Isn't it either way?
Depending?

The messenger isn't always killed.
Sometimes the Word is.
And so the greater the crime.

Life is what you make it.
Life is perception.
But Reality . . . Reality just is.

If I was given the power to be anyone I wanted to be in life, I'd be a philanthropist. So many of my life-long hopes and dreams of helping others faded due to a lack of means and the opposing ideals of one once closest to me.

Have you ever noticed that hatred is loaded with all sorts of ugly formations of the mind that weigh it down like crusty barnacles on the hull of the Soul? Deformities such as intolerance; prejudice; vengeance; separatism; arrogance of ethnicity, politics, or religion; and plain old ignorance which, by the way, is usually borne of one's choice to deny the wisdom of rationale.

And have you ever noticed how incredibly light and airy Love is? That, of itself, Love is as free as a butterfly and never weighted with negative attitudes? That it's pure? That Love's purity is unbounded? And that it can never leave negative karma in its wake?

What's even more interesting is that both are choices.

Unconditional Love is the happy homestead
of the joyous heart.
Wisdom is the shelter of serenity
for the enlightened mind.
Acceptance is the cozy cabin
of the peaceful soul.

The only way that you can give away your own power is if you choose to allow another to manipulate you through the voluntary surrender of those unique qualities and inherent rights which make you an independent individual.

Those who cannot envision Reality beyond the Establishment's prevailing ideology and opinion can never experience the wonder of breaking through the bonds of convention as a dreamer of possibilities so often does.

The Dreamwalkers. They are not made of the fluff of legend nor the mists of myth. They are the Ones who acutely perceive the quiet Knowing. They are the Ones whose footfalls follow the lead of their Souls.

The Tao of No-Eyes

The ones afflicted with spiritual paralysis saw
my old mentor through an array of multifaceted
lenses ground by the wheel of misperception.

Some focused only on her ethnicity.

Some centered solely on her predictions.

Some tinted her philosophy with personal
attitudes.

And some clouded her existence by their
lack of clarity of sight.

Yet there were those others.

Those others who instinctively knew.

They had the innate and inexplicable

Knowing that No~Eyes was an

embodiment of . . . the Tao of the Soul.

In troubled times, where do you turn?

To others?

Toward blame?

Search for sympathy?

Spin in circles chasing after reasons?

Rant and rave with explosive rage and anger?

Or go within where the peace of acceptance
awaits?

Nothing humbles me more than
the magnanimous splendor of Nature.
The unpretentious beauty of a lone wild-
flower is exquisite perfection.
And I, so aware of my own flawed
insignificance.

If I had to describe myself by comparing my Beingness to a type of fabric it wouldn't be silk or velvet. It wouldn't be satin or brocade. What comes to mind is Homespun.

I'm Homespun.

A well-known philosophical question is this:
Who are you?
I pose a deeper one:
Are any of us a Who at all?

Arrogance oft disguises ignorance
while meekness camouflages genius.

Contentment belongs to those who accept
their limitations and recognize the
alternate potentialities they open up.

Reality equals the unknowns
squared to the power of eight.
The fullest extent of Reality . . .
eights upon eights.

Henry David Thoreau once perceptively said, "It takes two to speak the truth—one to speak, and another to hear."

So many of you have heard.
So many of you have had the powerful Knowing come with that hearing. So many of you have had your subtle inner promptings confirmed and have experienced the wonderful sensation of having those much sought-after final verifications solidify your privately-held convictions.

To each and every single one of you—each one—I wish to heartfully express my deepest appreciation by saying, "Because you've heard through beautifully open and receiving hearts, because you've heard with the soul, you've been a sweet and most precious blessing to me. You've kept the sun shining brightly down upon my trail to illumine it with everlasting rays of receptivity. You have made it all—everything—so amazingly worthwhile. Consequently, because of that, you've left me with a sublime sense of inner contentment knowing that my small contributions to the human understanding of spiritual philosophy and the glimpses given into the true extent of Reality's unlimited potentialities have reached the end of their long journey.

Perhaps we'll meet again one day. And I suspect we will, you know. For alas, someone like me whose mind never stops being sparked by new ideas, is compelled to share them. Perhaps our paths will again converge as we meet while visiting some of those old familiar places—within the pages of a future novel or two. Though Woodsmoke was tentatively meant to mark the end of my nonfiction trail, life experiences have taught me the high wisdom of never, ever saying . . . "nevermore."

They came at me
   one by one.
Then two by two
   they came.
Soon there were scores
   as more joined more
   speeding through the air.

Circling. Circling.
Always circling, they
   wrapped themselves around me.

Swirling. Swirling.
Swirling into a mighty
   Force that pulsed with
   the Life of the Living Lights,
   that made a Shield of Prayer.

Thank you, my friends, for
   . . . all your encouragement
   . . . sending your prayers
   . . . hearing the words
   . . . and loving one another.

Hampton Roads Publishing Company

. . . for the evolving human spirit

Hampton Roads Publishing Company
publishes books on a variety of subjects including
metaphysics, health, complementary medicine,
visionary fiction, and other related topics.

For a copy of our latest catalog,
call toll-free, 800-766-8009,
or send your name and address to:

Hampton Roads Publishing Company, Inc.
1125 Stoney Ridge Road
Charlottesville, VA 22902
e-mail: hrpc@hrpub.com
www.hrpub.com